Introduction

Dear readers,
Thank you very much for choosing a book of the training assistance series of handball-uebungen.de.

Handball training for kiddies and young children is different from handball training for older players and considerably different from handball training for competitive players. During their first contact with "handball", kids should be familiarized with the ball in a playful way. They should be taught that being active, doing sports, playing together, and even playing against each other is fun.

This book contains a short introduction to handball for kiddies and young children and its special characteristics as well as example exercises which help to make your training units interesting and more diverse. Following this, there are five complete training units of different difficulty levels that focus on the basic handball techniques (dribbling, passing, catching, shooting, and defending in a game with opponents). The kids are playfully introduced to the subsequent handball-specific basics. At the same time, particular attention is payed to general physical experience and the development of coordination skills.

The exercises are illustrated and described in an easy, comprehensible manner. They can be immediately integrated in every training unit. By using the given training variants, you can easily adjust the difficulty level of the training units to the respective target group. The variants should also encourage you to modify and further develop the exercises to make each training unit a new and more diverse experience for the children.

Sample figure:

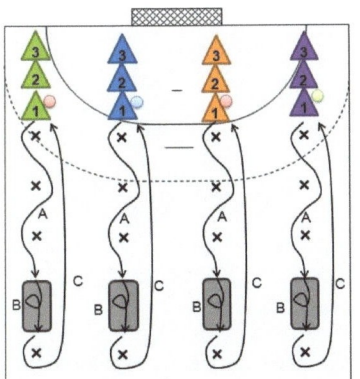

Contents

1. Basics of handball training for kiddies and young children Page 3
   - Different movement options   Page 3
   - Coordination basics   Page 4
   - Fun through games and competitions   Page 5
   - Use of various play toys   Page 5

2. Training unit explanations   Page 7
   - Difficulty level   Page 7
   - Structure of training units   Page 7

3. Training units   Page 8
   - M1: Coordination with balloons and handballs (⭐)   Page 8
   - M2: Dribbling (⭐⭐⭐)   Page 15
   - M3: Passing and catching (⭐⭐)   Page 21
   - M4: Shooting (⭐⭐)   Page 28
   - M5: Defending (⭐⭐⭐)   Page 34

4. Printing template for planning the training unit   Page 40

5. Editor´s note   Page 41

6. Further reference books published by DV Concept   Page 42

Acknowledgments
Writing this book would not have been possible without the help of Alie Lackner who contributed to the training units by sharing her experience in the field of children's gymnastics, by coming up with game ideas, and by giving plenty of advice regarding age-appropriate exercising. Thank you so much for this. I also wish to thank my co-editor, Elke Lackner, who made a major contribution regarding the concept and structure of the training units and exercises.

1st English edition released on 20 Apr 2016
German original edition released on 20 Jun 2014

Published by DV Concept
Editors, Design and Layout: Jörg Madinger, Elke Lackner
Proofreading and English translation: Nina-Maria Nahlenz

ISBN: 978-3-95641-167-0

The book and its contents are protected by copyright. No reprinting, photomechanical reproduction, storing or processing in electronic systems without the publisher's written permission.

1. Basics of minihandball training and handball training for young kids

The primary objective of minihandball is to give children the fun of sports and to provide an opportunity to learn, try out and apply different (all-kind-of-sports) movements. The sports lessons should be organized in an entertaining and exciting manner though, giving each child the opportunity to get involved. Children have a strong urge to do physical activities and to play and they want to satisfy this urge during the sports lessons.

Hence, the following rules should be observed when planning and supervising a training unit.

Different movement options:
The children aged 5 to 9 years are in the best age for learning motor skills, i.e., they learn movements and movement patterns quickly and easily. Hence, it is important to provide them with plenty of opportunities to gain movement experiences. However, the children should not only try out handball-specific movements but all-kind-of-sports movements as well. Simple activity courses create good opportunities to combine movement sequences.

Example exercise:

B1	Continued movement	10	10

Setting:
- Put a bench on the floor and place two cones on top; put gym mats on the floor behind the bench.
- The players line up, with the last player holding a handball.
- Two players stand in the playing field (here 6 and 7).

Course:
- The players stand in the line with their legs spread, facing 5.
- The backmost player (5) hands over the ball through his legs to 4, who hands over the ball through his legs to 3, and so on until the ball has arrived 1 (A).

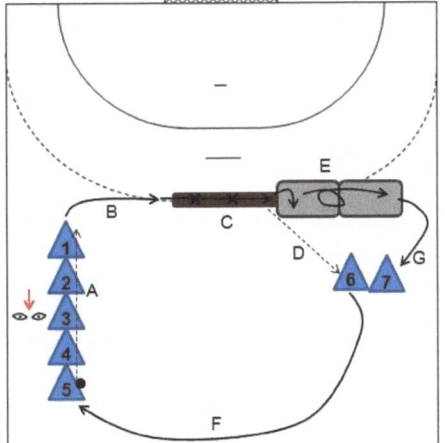

- ① turns around, runs towards the bench while holding the ball (B), steps onto the bench and balances his way across it, climbing over the cones (C). Once he has arrived at the end, ① passes the ball to ⑥ (D).
- Following the pass, ① jumps down from the bench and does a somersault (forward roll, sideways roll) on the mats (E).
- ⑥ runs towards the line of players, turns around (F), and starts the course over by handing over the ball through his legs to ⑤.
- ① lines up behind ⑦ (G).

And so on.

Coordination basics

Coordination basics are an important prerequisite to learning and performing specific movements accurately, also at a higher age. Hence, handball training for children focuses particularly on the development of coordination skills, such as rhythmic skills, orientation, balance, reaction, differentiation (adjust movements to different situations), and movement combination.

Example exercises:

B2	Balance: Balancing across benches	10	10

Setting:
- Put benches on the floor (upside down, if applicable). Alternatively, you can put ropes on the floor.

Course:
- Two children (one child on each end of the bench) start balancing across the bench at the same time.
- Once they have arrived the middle part of the bench, they try to go past each other without stepping down.
- The players should help each other, though.

B3	Differentiation: Dribbling with different balls	10	10

Course:
- Each player gets a ball (basketball, tennis ball, handball, foam ball).
- The players crisscross through the court and dribble their ball.
- On the coach's command, the players exchange their ball with one of the players who is dribbling another type of ball. Afterwards, the players start over by dribbling their new ball.

| B4 | Rhythm, orientation | 10 | 10 |

Setting:
- Put four gym mats on the floor with three hoops in front of each mat. The players stand on the mats.

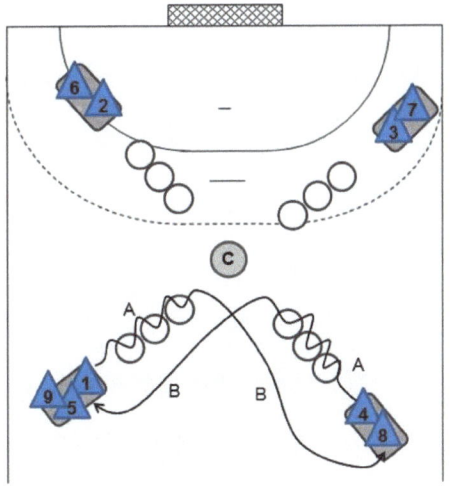

Course:
- The coach in the center points at two mats.
- The first players of the two respective mats leave their mat and jump through the hoop line with both feet (A).
- Afterwards, they line up behind the players at the respective other mat (B).
- Once the players have arrived at the end of the hoop line, the coach points at two other mats and the next two players start.

Fun through games and competitions

The children should be given the opportunity to satisfy their urge to play and to let off steam. However, joy of playing and fun are most important.
Through short games, the children also learn to follow the simple rules of game and fair play. Likewise, the children develop team spirit. The following training units consist of numerous short games and competitions that can be applied variably.

Use of various play toys

Children have an awful lot of fun in training units that are organized in an entertaining way. Creativity knows no boundaries here. Plenty of household objects may serve as play toys, e.g. throwing pouches made of washing mitts filled with peas, beer mats, balloons, paper cups, handkerchiefs, etc.

Example exercises:

| B5 | Beer mat game | 10 | 10 |

Setting:
- Spread beer mats across the whole court.
- Make teams.

Course:
- The first players of each team start in parallel and each pick up one beer mat from the floor.
- They exchange a high-five with the next player who then also picks up a beer mat.
- The entire team builds a tower using the beer mats their teammates picked up.
- Which team has built the highest tower in the end?

| B6 | Paper cups and tennis balls | 10 | 10 |

Course:
- Each child gets a paper cup and a tennis ball.
- The children throw their tennis ball in the air and try to catch it with the paper cup.
- The children balance their tennis ball on top of their paper cup (which is upside down) and run through a course (slalom run around cones, climb over small vaulting boxes, etc.).

2. Training unit explanations

Difficulty level

The training units are divided into three difficulty levels:

    Age: 4 years and older – The exercises of this training unit can be done by any child and without any basic skills.

    Age: 6 years and older – Basically, the training units can be done by any child, however, certain motor skills are prerequisite. Variants offer the opportunity to modify the difficulty level in the training units.

   Age: 7 years and older – These training units partially require that the players already have gained experience regarding the basic skills (dribbling, passing, catching). Variants also offer the opportunity to modify the difficulty level in the training units.

Structure of training units

The training units each deal with a topic that serves as the golden thread. Nevertheless, the children ought to be introduced to the topics in a playful way. Between the games, basic exercises provide the children with the opportunity to try out, practice, and vary the techniques. The training units each start with a short warm-up and then move on to games and exercises focusing on the respective topic. The training unit is closed by a game variant in which the delivered contents can be applied.

The training units are intended for a total training time of 60 minutes. If there is more time available, extending the individual exercises and games or trying out the numerous variants would be a good idea.

Children have a fertile imagination, therefore, little stories may help to catch their attention and to improve their understanding, especially in children of beginner age. The training units contain some examples.

3. Training units

No.: M1		Coordination with balloons and handballs		☆	60	
Opening part		**Main part**		**Final part**		
X	Warm-up/running	X	Ball handling/coordination	X	Closing game	
	Running exercise		Passing and catching		Sprint contest	
	Short game		Dribbling			
X	Coordination	X	Shooting			
	Sprint contest		Defending			
X	Strengthening		Goalkeeper			
	Ball familiarization		Applying contents in a game			

Key:

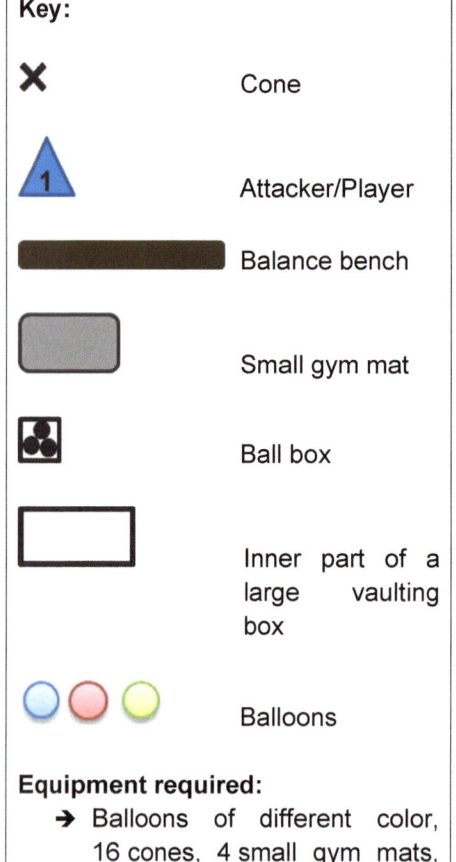

- Cone
- Attacker/Player
- Balance bench
- Small gym mat
- Ball box
- Inner part of a large vaulting box
- Balloons

Equipment required:
→ Balloons of different color, 16 cones, 4 small gym mats, 4 balance benches, 2 inner parts of a large vaulting box, 2 ball boxes with sufficient number of handballs

Description:
Besides handballs, this training unit features balloons as small play toys. The warm-up and strengthening exercises allow the children to familiarize with the balloon before they have to fulfill different tasks with it in a competition that includes coordination elements. Afterwards, there is a shooting exercise in which the children use the handball while the balloons serve as targets. Following a handball course, there will be a closing game in which both play toys will be used in an equal manner.

The training unit consists of the following key exercises:
- Warm-up/stretching (individual exercise: 10 minutes/total time: 10 minutes)
- Age-specific strengthening exercise (5/15)
- Competition game with coordination (10/25)
- Shooting exercise (10/35)
- Coordination course with shooting (10/45)
- Closing game with two variants (15/60)

Training unit total time: 60 minutes

| No.: M1-1 | Warm-up/running | 10 | 10 |

Setting:
- Each player gets a balloon. Teams are made using the different balloon colors.

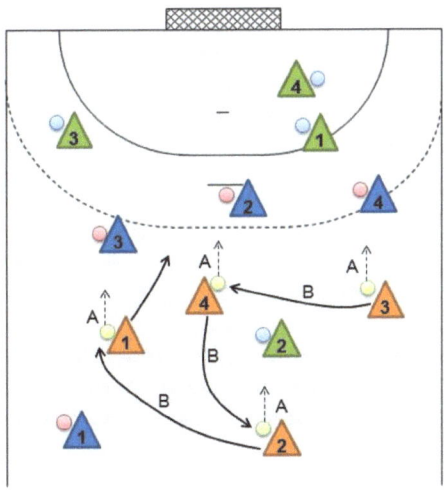

Basic course:
- The players crisscross throughout the court according to one of the variants below, keeping their balloon in the air.
- As soon as the coach calls out a balloon color, the players who have a balloon of the respective color throw it in the air as high as they can (A) and then try to catch one of the other balloons of the same color (B).
- Afterwards, the players crisscross throughout the court again and the coach calls out further colors.

Running variants:
- The players keep pushing their balloon slightly in the air and follow it so that it won't touch the ground.
- The players try to control their balloon with one hand, but without holding it.
- The players keep their balloon in the air with the head.
- The players keep their balloon in the air by touching it with a different part of the body each time it comes down (with the hand, head, elbow, foot ...).

| No.: M1-2 | Age-specific strengthening exercise | 5 | 15 |

Course:
- Each player has a balloon again.
- The players crawl on all fours and roll their balloon over the floor by touching it slightly with their arms or legs.
- The players lie on the floor face-down winding like a snake while pushing the balloon forward with their head.
- The players do backward crab movements (on their hands and feet with the belly facing upwards and the bottom downwards) throughout the court and try to balance the balloon on their belly.

Story for the strengthening exercise:
- It is springtime and there are a lot of insects romping about on the meadow. All the insects want to collect nesting materials.
- The children are little bugs and romp about throughout the court on all fours, carrying their materials.
- The children are earthworms and carry their materials without using their arms and legs.
- The children are spiders and carry their materials while doing crab movements.

| No.: M1-3 | Competition game with coordination | 10 | 25 |

Setting:
- Make teams of 3 to 4 players with one balloon per team.
- Put cones and mats on the floor as shown in the figure.

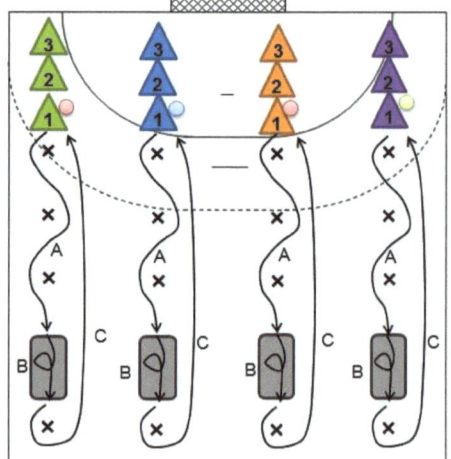

Course:
- The first players each start and run a slalom around the cones while carrying the balloon, however, without holding it (A), but rather by pushing it slightly forward or controlling it with the palm of their hand.
- Once they have arrived the mat, the players throw their balloon in the air,

- do a 360° turn-around; and catch the balloon coming down (B).
- Afterwards, they hold their balloon in their hands, run back along the line of cones as fast as they can, and finally hand over the balloon to the next player (C).
- The group which has finished the course first receives a point.
- Which group has the most points after several courses?

Variants for further courses:
- The balloon must not be controlled, but rather be pushed forward.
- The balloon must be controlled with the head/foot.
- Once they have arrived the mat, the players throw their balloon in the air, sit down and get up again before catching the balloon coming down.

No.: M1-4	Shooting exercise	10	35

Setting:
- Position benches in such a way that you get a square. Fill the square with balloons.

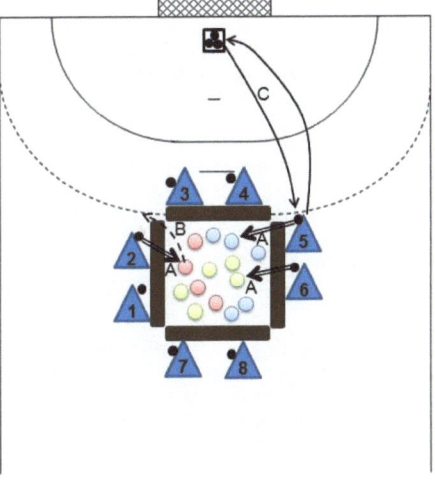

Course:
- The players stand around the playing field, each player holding a handball.
- The players try to shoot the balloons inside the square (A) in such a way that they burst or jump out of the square (B).
- The players pick up the handballs bouncing out of the playing field in order to shoot again.
- If a handball remains inside the square, the player fetches a new one from the ball box (C).
- The group tries to remove as many balloons from the playing field as they can within a defined time period.

| No.: M1-5 | Coordination course with shooting | 10 | 45 |

Setting:
- Put inner parts of a large vaulting box on the floor and place one gym mat inside each.
- Position a bench straight behind.
- Put cones on the floor in order to define the shooting line and position another bench at some meters' distance to the wall.
- Make two groups. The first player (1) of each group stands between the mat and the bench.

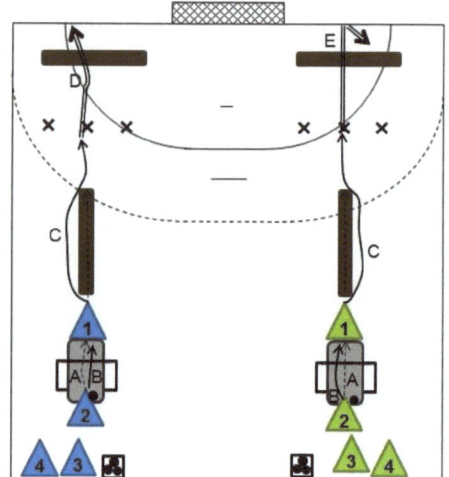

Course:
- 2 passes or rolls the ball through the vaulting box part to 1 (A).
- Afterwards, 2 crawls through the vaulting box part and takes over the position of 1 (B).
- 1 picks up the ball, runs along the bench and rolls the ball on top of it (C).
- Once he has arrived the cones, 1 either throws a bounce pass (D) or a straight pass (E) at the wall so that the ball remains behind the bench.
- As soon as 1 has rolled his ball across the bench, 3 starts rolling/passing the ball to 2 (A).
- And so on.

Variants (depending on the level of performance):
- Balancing across the bench and moving the ball around the body in circles.
- Balancing across the bench and rolling/kicking the ball on the bench.
- Balancing across the bench and holding the ball above the head while climbing over cones on the bench.
- Balancing across the bench and dribbling the ball on the bench/on the side of the bench.

⚠ If the ball falls down while rolling it, the player may put it back onto the bench on the very same spot where he lost it.

Doing the course as a competition:
- Balls that remain behind the bench are kept there. If the player misses, he picks up the ball again and starts over with the same ball as soon as it is his turn again. Which group has an empty ball box first?

Minihandball training and handball training for young kids

| No.: M1-6 | Closing game | 15 | 60 |

Setting:
- Divide the court in two halves using benches.
- Put the same number of balloons and balls on each side of the playing field.
- Make two teams, with one team on each side.

Course:
- On command, both teams start in parallel.
- The players pick up a ball or a balloon (A) and throw it to the other side (B and C).
- The coach whistles after 2 to 3 minutes.
- Both teams stop throwing and the coach counts the balls/balloons on each side. The team that has fewer balls/balloons on their side wins the course.
- Which team has won the game after several courses?

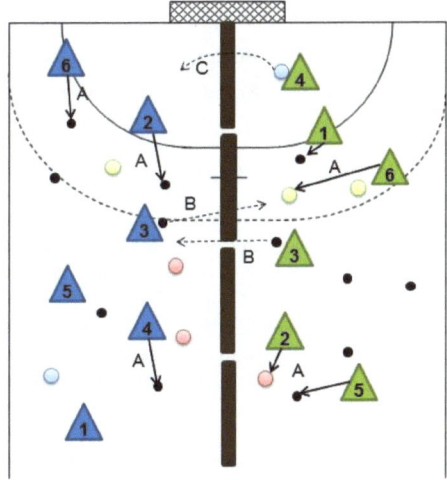

Figure: Variant 1

Extension:
- Put an empty ball box on each side of the playing field. One player of each team stands in the opponents' half.
- Once the coach has whistled, the players pick up a ball or balloon again (A) and throw it to the other side (B/C).
- The player on the opponents' half may pick up balls and balloons, too (D), and puts them into the ball box (E). The balls/balloons in the ball box may not be used or thrown anymore. When counting, the balls/balloons in the box are added to the balls/balloons lying on the respective half of the playing field.

Figure: Variant 2

Story for the game:
- The balls and balloons are garbage. Two villages want to get rid of their garbage. The inhabitants meet at night and secretly throw their garbage into the other village. Unfortunately, the inhabitants of both villages have the same idea. Well, let's see who is more successful.

⚠ Each player may pick up only one ball/balloon at a time.

⚠ Each player must throw his ball/balloon to the other side himself. The balls and balloons may not be handed over to teammates.

Notes:

Minihandball training and handball training for young kids

No.: M2		Dribbling		★★★	60	
Opening part		**Main part**		**Final part**		
X	Warm-up/running	X	Ball handling/coordination	X	Closing game	
	Running exercise		Passing and catching		Sprint contest	
X	Short game	X	Dribbling			
X	Coordination		Shooting			
	Sprint contest		Defending			
	Strengthening		Goalkeeper			
	Ball familiarization		Applying contents in a game			

Key:

✕   Cone

▲1   Attacker/Player

●1   Defending player

▬   Balance bench

⬛   Ball box

◯   Hoop

●   Foam ball

◆   Dice

Equipment required:
→ 1 hoop per player (at least 8), 13 cones, 2 foam balls, 2 balance benches, 2 foam dices, 2 ball boxes with sufficient number of handballs, 2 pens, paper sheets

Description:
The objective of the training unit is to improve ball handling when dribbling. The warm-up already focuses on dribbling and includes different variants of dribbling. Following a short game and a coordination exercise, there will be an exercise during which the players must take into account external factors when dribbling the ball. In a competition game that includes dribbling coordination and during a ball transportation game at the end of the unit, the players are to apply and enhance the new skills.

The training unit consists of the following key exercises:
- Warm-up/running (individual exercise: 10 minutes/total time: 10 minutes)
- Short game (10/20)
- Coordination exercise (5/25)
- Dribbling exercise with shooting (10/35)
- Dribbling coordination (10/45)
- Closing game with two variants (15/60)

Training unit total time: 60 minutes

| No.: M2-1 | Warm-up/running | 10 | 10 |

Setting:
- Put some cones on the floor of the court outside of the 9-meter zone.

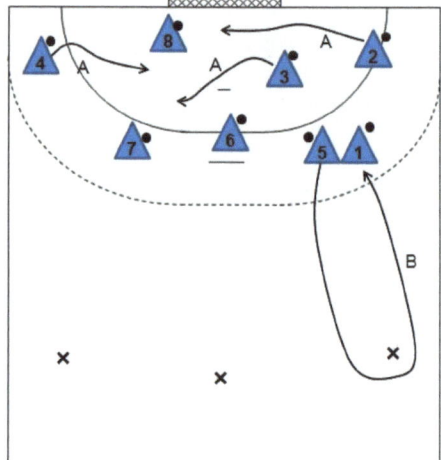

Course:
- Each player has a ball. The players crisscross throughout the 9-meter zone (A) and practice different dribbling variants (dribbling with the throwing hand/the non-throwing hand/both hands alternately).
- As soon as the coach calls out two names, the two respective players take each other by the hand and run around one of the cones together (B).
- Depending on the level of performance:
    o The players hold their ball in their hands while running around the cones.
    o One of the players dribbles his ball.
    o Both players dribble their ball.

| No.: M2-2 | Short game | 10 | 20 |

Setting:
- Spread hoops across the court.
- Each child stands in a hoop.
- One child is without a hoop (1).
- The children are assigned fruits (apples, peas ...), e.g. by picking cards showing fruits.

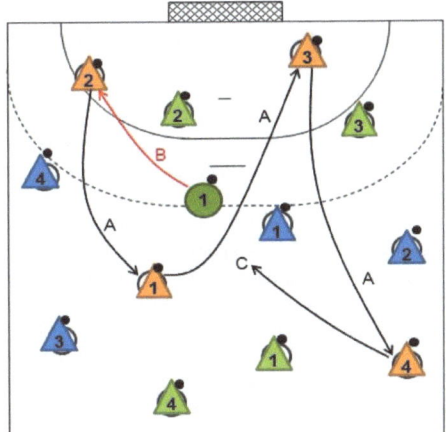

Course:
- The player without a hoop (1) calls out a fruit aloud (e.g. "apples").
- All children assigned to this type of fruit must swap hoops. They dribble out of their hoop and into one of the free hoops (A).
- (1) also dribbles and tries to get one of the free hoops (B).
- If (1) succeeds, he becomes one of the fruits. The player who is without a hoop now (C) gives the next command.
- On the command "fruit salad", all players must swap hoops.

Variants:
- The players do not have handballs, i.e. they play the game without dribbling.
- There are hoops of different color. The hoop color indicates the type of fruit. On the command "fruit salad", the players hence become another type of fruit.

| No.: M2-3 | Coordination | 5 | 25 |

Course:
- Each player has a handball and stands on the court, keeping a certain distance to the other players.
- Depending on the level of performance, the players try out the following exercises:
    - They dribble their handball with both hands alternately.
    - They dribble their handball around their body.
    - They dribble their handball while sitting down.
    - They dribble their handball and try to bounce it through their legs while making a large forward step.
    - They dribble their handball in front of their body, do a 360° turn-around, and keep dribbling afterwards.

| No.: M2-4 | Dribbling exercise with shooting | 10 | 35 |

Setting:
- Position 3 to 4 cone goals with one defending player per goal.
- Define a shooting line using two cones and put a bench on the floor with cones on top.

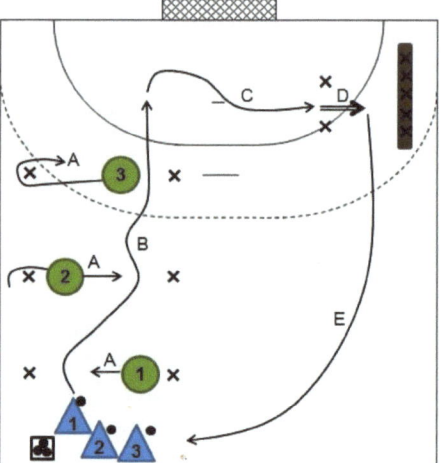

Course:
- The defending players sidestep around the cones, facing the goal (with their backs turned to the attacking players) (A).
- The defending players start at different times and in different directions.
- ① dribbles through the cone goals (B). He has to avoid a collision with the sidestepping defending players.
- Once ① has run through the last cone goal, ② starts.
- As soon as ① has run through the last cone goal, he turns right, dribbles towards the shooting line (C) and eventually shoots (D). ① tries to hit a cone. If he succeeds, he gets a point (the cone must be put back on the bench).
- Once all attacking players have run through the cone goals once, the defending players are changed.
- Which player has the most points after everybody has played defense once?

⚠ At first, the defending players should keep their pace. They also should not react to the attacking players so that the attacking players can anticipate the defending players' running moves. Allow a change of pace during the course, if appropriate.

⚠ The attacking players should make out and use the gaps. Ideally, they dribble through the cone goals without being touched by a defending player.

⚠ The difficulty level of the exercise can be adjusted by changing the goal size.

| No.: M2-5 | Dribbling coordination | 10 | 45 |

Setting:
- Make two or more teams.
- Put benches and hoops on the floor, as shown in the figure.
- Put one foam dice (or small dice) per team behind the line of hoops.
- Each group gets a pen as well as a paper sheet with the numbers 1 to 6 written largely on it.

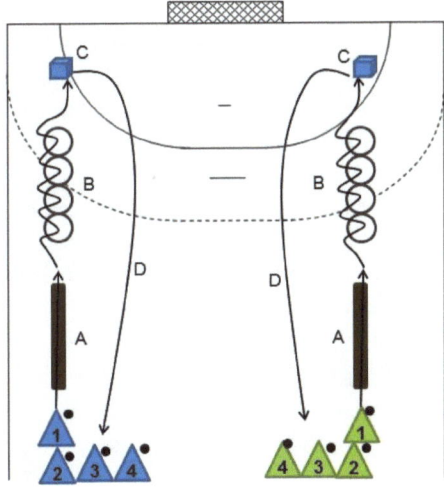

Course:
- The first players start in parallel.
- They dribble their handball on the bench while running along the bench (A).
- Afterwards, they bounce their handball once into each hoop (B). While doing this, they run along the line of hoops.
- At the end, the players roll their dice (C), run back, and exchange a high-five with the next player (D). The number of points on the respective dice may be crossed out on the paper sheet.
- Which team has crossed out the 6 numbers first?

Variants on the bench (depending on the level of performance):
- The players run across the bench and bounce their handball on the bench several times, but take it up after each bounce.
- The players run across the bench and dribble their handball on it (without taking it up).
- The players run across the bench and dribble their handball on the floor.
- The players run along the bench and dribble their handball on the other side of the bench.

⚠️ The course is not about speed. The players should do the exercise properly and – if possible – neither lose their handball nor take it up.

| No.: M2-6 | Closing game | 15 | 60 |

Setting:
- Put a ball box on each side of the playing field. Each ball box contains the same number of handballs.
- Define the playing field boundary with cones.
- Make two teams and assign a ball box to each team.

Course – variant 1:
- On command, both teams start in parallel.
- Each player picks up a handball from the ball box of his team (A), then dribbles to the other side (B), and puts the handball into the opponents' ball box (C).

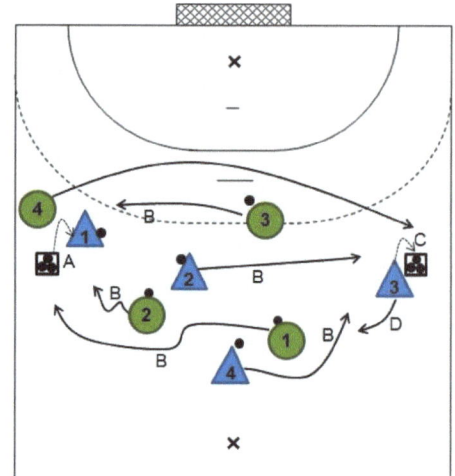

Figure: Variant 1

- Afterwards, the players run back without a ball (D) and pick up the next ball from their own box.
- The coach whistles after a defined time period (about 3 to 5 minutes). The players stand still and the coach counts the balls in the ball boxes. The team that has the fewest balls in their box receives a point for this course.
- Which team has scored highest after several courses?

Extension (variant 2):
- The course remains the same as for variant 1.
- One player of each team has a foam ball. This player tries to shoot at the dribbling opponents (E).
- Once a player has been hit, he first has to dribble around the cone defining the playing field boundary before he may continue dribbling towards the opponents' ball box (F).

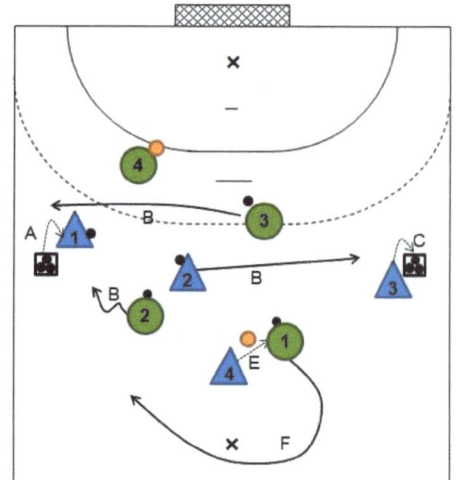

⚠ Each player may dribble only one ball at a time to the other side.

Figure: Variant 2

⚠ Each player must dribble to the other side himself. The players are not allowed to hand over or pass their handballs.

Minihandball training and handball training for young kids

No.: M3			Passing and catching			★★	60	
Opening part			**Main part**			**Final part**		
X	Warm-up/running			Ball handling/coordination		X	Closing game	
	Running exercise		X	Passing and catching			Sprint contest	
X	Short game			Dribbling				
	Coordination			Shooting				
	Sprint contest			Defending				
	Strengthening			Goalkeeper				
X	Ball familiarization		X	Applying contents in a game				

Key:

✕	Cone
▲1	Attacker/Player
●1	Defending player
▬	Balance bench
▢	Small vaulting box
⚫⚫⚫	Ball box
▭	Large vaulting box, open
☐	Small vaulting box, upside down
○	Hoop

Equipment required:
→ 7 hoops, 4 small vaulting boxes, 4 balance benches, 1 game of pairs, 2 large vaulting boxes, 8 cones, sufficient number of handballs

Description:
The objective of the training unit is to improve passing and catching. The warm-up already involves passing before the players will try out and practice different passing variants. In a short competition game and the consecutive passing exercise with timekeeping, proper passing and catching will be rewarded. At the end, two playing variants offer the opportunity to practice passing in game situations.

The training unit consists of the following key exercises:
- Warm-up/running (individual exercise: 10 minutes/total time: 10 minutes)
- Ball familiarization (5/15)
- Short game (15/30)
- Passing exercise (5/35)
- Short game with passing and defending (15/50)
- Closing game (10/60)

Training unit total time: 60 minutes

| No.: M3-1 | Warm-up/running | 10 | 10 |

Setting:
- The players stand in a circle, one player standing in the center and holding a handball.
- If there is a large number of players, form several circles. The exercise can be done in parallel.

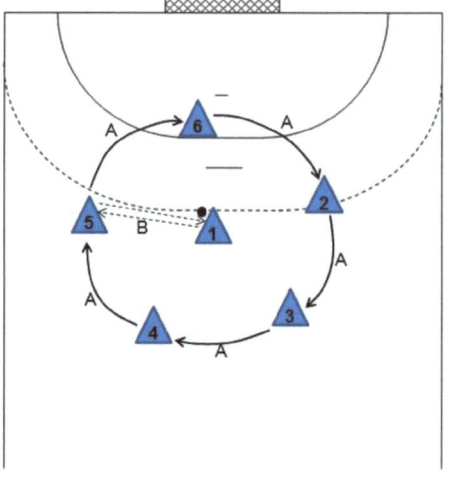

Basic course:
- The players move round in a circle at a slow, steady pace (A).
- The player in the center calls out a name and then plays a double pass with the respective player (B).
- The group keeps moving round in the circle. The player in the center calls out another name and once more plays a double pass.
- After several passes, change the player in the center.
- Change the running variants for the players moving round in the circle (forward, backward, hopping, sidestepping to the right or left).
- Instruct the players to do passing variants when playing the double pass (bounce pass, direct pass, chest pass, over-the-head pass).

⚠️ The player in the center should wait until he has made eye contact with the other player before playing the pass (B).

⚠️ The running players should maintain the circle form and also keep the distance to the player in front. So the challenge is to pay attention to the player in front and to adjust the pace accordingly.

Minihandball training and handball training for young kids

| No.: M3-2 | Ball familiarization | 5 | 15 |

Course:
- Two players make a team and stand face-to-face at a distance of 2 to 3 meters, each team having one handball.
- The two players pass the ball. Depending on the level of performance, the players try out the following passing variants:
    - Bounce pass with the throwing hand, the non-throwing hand
    - Chest pass
    - Direct pass with the throwing hand, non-throwing hand
    - The player turns his back towards his teammate and plays a two-handed pass over the head.
    - The player turns his back towards his teammate and passes through his straddled legs.
    - One player is standing, the other one is sitting while passing.

| No.: M3-3 | Short game | 15 | 30 |

Setting:
- Put a game of pairs (5 to 8 pairs) upside down on top of a small vaulting box.
- Put 7 hoops on the floor in front of the small box (see figure).
- For course 1, define the positions with cones, if necessary.
- Make two teams. The players of one team stand in a zig-zag pattern (see figure), with the first player holding a handball. The other team starts in front of the hoops.

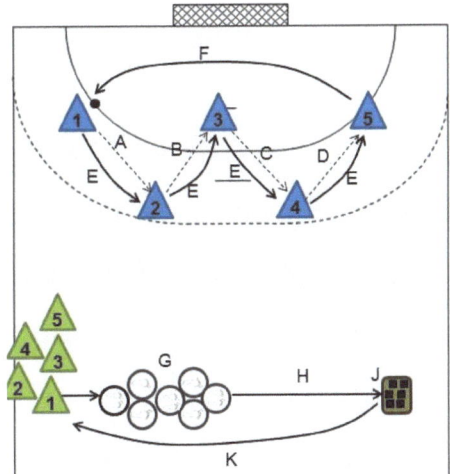

Course of team 1:
- On the starting signal, 1 passes the ball to 2 (A). Afterwards, 2 passes the ball to 3 (B), 3 to 4 (C), and 4 to 5 (D).
- Once they have played the pass, the players take over the position they passed to (E).
- As soon as 5 has received the ball, he runs towards the start position of 1 (F) and starts the course over by passing the ball.
- The team counts how often the course starts over from the start position.
- They may keep playing until the second team has fulfilled their task (game of pairs).

Course of team 2:
- On the starting signal, the first player starts jumping through the line of hoops (with both feet into the single hoops and with one foot each into the double hoops) (G) and then runs towards the small vaulting box (H).
- Once he has arrived, he flips two cards of the game of pairs (J). If the cards match, he takes them with him to the group. If they do not match, he puts them back (upside down) and runs back without cards (K).
- Afterwards, the next player starts. The team keeps playing until they have solved the game of pairs.

Overall course:
- On command, both teams start their task in parallel.
- Once team 2 has solved the game of pairs, they shout out "Stop" and the points of team 1 are recorded.
- Afterwards, the teams switch tasks.
- Which team has managed to play the most rounds in the passing game?

Passing variants:
- Bounce passes only
- Direct passes only
- Bounce passes and direct passes alternately

Minihandball training and handball training for young kids

| No.: M3-4 | Passing exercise | 5 | 35 |

Setting:
- Make two teams. The teammates stand face-to-face in groups of 2 on two benches at a distance of 2 to 3 meters.

Course:
- The groups of 2 each pass a ball (A).
- They play the following passing variants:
    - Bounce passes (A)
    - Direct passes (B)
    - Chest passes (C)

Variant (D):
- The teams each pass only one ball.
- 1 passes the ball to 2, 2 to 3, 3 to 4, and so on until the last player gets the ball (here 6). The last player starts passing the ball back to 5 and the players pass the ball back until 1 gets the ball again.
- Which team has been fastest in passing the ball from 1 to 6 and back?

⚠ The players should play proper passes so that their teammates are able to catch the ball without stepping down from the bench.

Minihandball training and handball training for young kids

| No.: M3-5 | Short game with passing and defending | 15 | 50 |

Setting:
- Divide the court into three playing fields using cones or lines and make three teams.
- Position a ball box and three empty boxes as shown in the figure.

Course:
- 1, 2, and 3 play together with 4, 5, and 6.
- 1, 2, and 3 pick up the balls from the ball box (A) and then play a bounce pass (B) or a direct pass (C) to 4, 5, or 6 who put the balls into their box (D).
- 1, 2, and 3 try to steal the ball (E) and put it into one of the boxes on the side (F).
- Once all balls have been passed, count the balls of the defending players and the attacking players each (the points of the attacking players count for both attacking teams). Afterwards, the teams change tasks.
- Which team has the most points after three rounds (passing, catching, defending)?

⚠ The players should avoid playing banana passes. For each clear banana pass, the defending players may get a point.

⚠ Each player has to pass his ball to the other side himself. The players may not hand over the balls within a playing field.

| No.: M3-6 | Closing game | 10 | 60 |

Setting:
- Position two large, open vaulting boxes in front of two opposite walls.
- Put a small box each in front of the large boxes at some meters' distance.
- At the beginning, one player per team stands on the respective small box.

Course:
- The players of the team in ball possession try to pass the ball to the player on the small box by moving and passing (A and B) in a well-coordinated manner.
- If the player on the box catches the ball, he tries to bounce the ball into the open box (C). He may also bounce the ball against the wall.
- If the player strikes, the coach passes a new ball to the former defending team (D). If the player misses, the players keep playing with the same ball, however, both teams are allowed to secure it.
- Change the player on the box after each shooting attempt.
- Which team strikes more often?

⚠ The shooting player may not be attacked during the shot. The players are not allowed to steal or block the ball that is being shot at the large box.

Notes:

No.: M4		Shooting		★★	60
Opening part		**Main part**		**Final part**	
	Warm-up/stretching		Ball handling/coordination	X	Closing game
	Running exercise		Passing and catching		Sprint contest
X	Short game		Dribbling		
	Coordination	X	Shooting		
	Sprint contest		Defending		
	Strengthening		Goalkeeper		
X	Ball familiarization		Applying contents in a game		

Key:
- ✗ Cone
- 🔺1 Attacker/Player
- 🟢1 Defending player
- ▬ Large safety mat, upright
- ▭ Large vaulting box
- ▫ Small vaulting box
- Ball box
- 🟠 Medicine ball
- ⭕ Hoop

Equipment required:
➔ 5 medicine balls, 2 hoops, tape, 1 large vaulting box, 1 small vaulting box, 10 cones, 2 large safety mats, 2 ball boxes with sufficient number of handballs

Description:
This training unit focuses on shooting at non-moving and moving targets. Following a short tag game for warm-up and a short ball familiarization game, the players first practice their shooting accuracy during a shooting competition and afterwards during a circle training with different non-moving targets and a shot at the goal.

The training unit is rounded off with a closing game that includes shooting with two goalkeepers.

The training unit consists of the following key exercises:
- Short game (10/10)
- Ball familiarization (10/20)
- Shooting competition (10/30)
- Shooting circle training (20/50)
- Closing game (10/60)

Training unit total time: 60 minutes

| No.: M4-1 | Short game | 10 | 10 |

Setting:
- Define the start and finish line with cones or lines.

Course:
- One player is the tagger (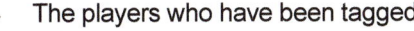) who stands in the center of the playing field (figure 1).
- He gives the command "Spider, come out of your house!".
- This is the sign for the other children to sprint across the playing field until they have crossed the other line (A).
- The tagger tries to tag one or more players (B).
- The players who have been tagged ( in the figure) remain standing in the field.
- Afterwards, the tagger calls out the command one more time (figure 2) and the players sprint across the playing field again (C). The tagger, who may move freely throughout the playing field (E), but also the players that have been tagged before may now tag the other players (D). These players () must stand on the spot where they have been tagged, however, they may move their upper body and arms. In this way, the field narrows more and more (see figure 3).

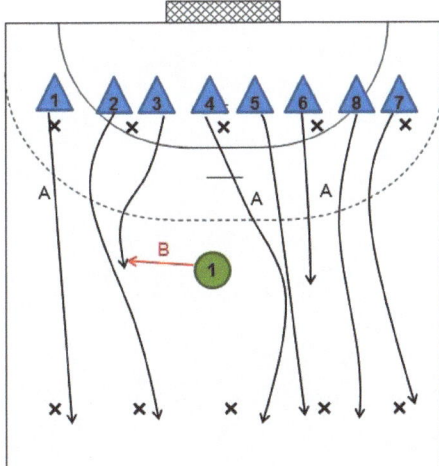

Figure 1

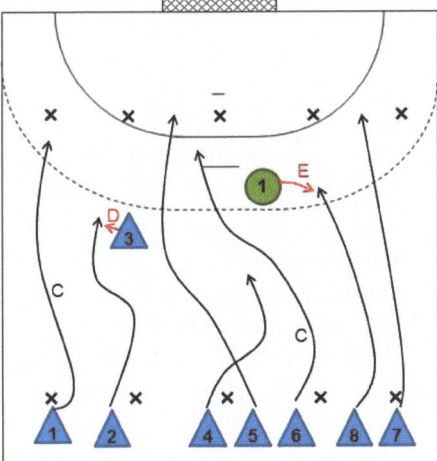

Figure 2

The last player tagged becomes the tagger in the next round.

Figure 3

No.: M4-2	Ball familiarization		10	20

Setting:
- Make two teams and fill a ball box for each team with the same number of handballs.

Course:
- One player of each team starts at the ball box. He throws the balls from the box into the playing field (A, B, and C) in order to empty the box.
- The opponents pick up the balls (D) and put them back into the box (E).
- The coach whistles after 2 minutes and counts the number of balls in each box.
- The team which has the fewest balls in the box receives a point.
- Afterwards, the course starts over with new players at the ball boxes.

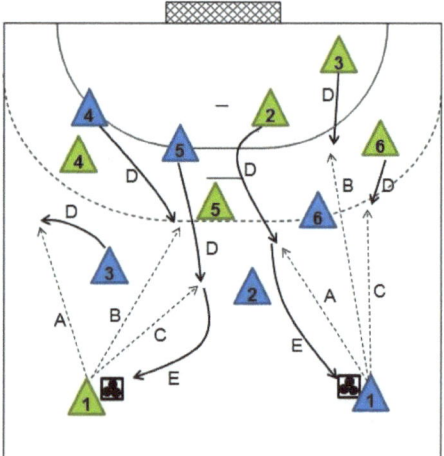

⚠ If possible, each player should try to empty the ball box once. If there is a large number of players, two players empty the box together.

| No.: M4-3 | Shooting competition | 10 | 30 |

Setting:
- Make two teams. The players of each team stand on the side line of a playing field defined with cones or lines (see figure).
- Put medicine balls in the center of the playing field.

Course:
- Each player has a handball.
- On command, both teams start and try to move the medicine balls across the opponents' line by aiming and shooting their handballs at the medicine balls.
- The players may all shoot at the same time and at all the medicine balls.
- Once a medicine ball has crossed one of the lines completely, the players must not shoot at this medicine ball anymore.
- Which team has moved the most medicine balls into the opponents' playing field in the end?

⚠ Adjust the distance between the lines and the medicine balls to the players' level of performance.

| No.: M4-4 | Shooting circle training | 20 | 50 |

Setting:

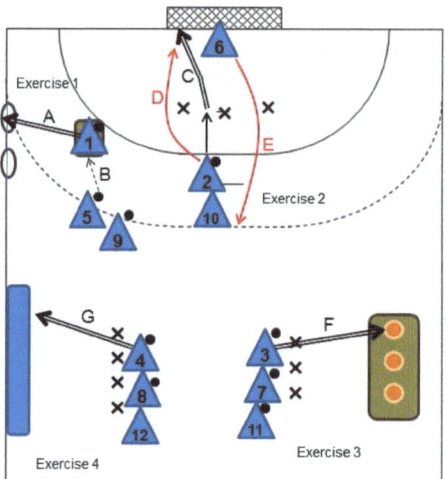

- Exercise 1: Use tape to attach two hoops to the wall at different heights. Position a small vaulting box in front of the wall at some meters' distance.
- Exercise 2: Use cones to define a shooting line at about 4 meters' distance to the goal.
- Exercise 3: Put medicine balls on top of a large vaulting box. Use cones to define a shooting line.
- Exercise 4: Position a large safety mat upright on the wall. Use tape to define targets in the corners. Define the shooting line with cones.

Basic course:

- Make groups of 3 to 4 players. The groups each go to one of the exercise zones.
- On command, the groups start doing the tasks of the respective exercise.
- After about four minutes, the groups change the exercise zones. Repeat until each group has done each exercise once.

Exercise 1:

- One player (1) sits on the small vaulting box and tries to hit a hoop (A).
- The other players pass additional balls (B).
- Change tasks after five shots.

Exercise 2:

- One player starts as the goalkeeper (6).
- The other players shoot from the shooting line and try to score by bouncing the ball into the goal (C).
- If a player scores, he becomes the new goalkeeper (D) and the former goalkeeper lines up for shooting (E).

Exercise 3:

- The three players shoot from the line one after another and try to hit the medicine balls so that they fall down from the box. They keep shooting until no medicine balls are left on the box. (F).

Exercise 4:
- The three players stand behind the line and shoot at the large safety mat one after another. They try to hit each of the taped corners at least once (G).

⚠️ The exercises are not about time but about proper performance. Therefore, correct the shooting technique and show how to improve it again and again.

No.: M4-5	Closing game	10	60

Setting:
- Position one large safety mat as target on each side of the playing field and define the shooting lines with cones (see figure).

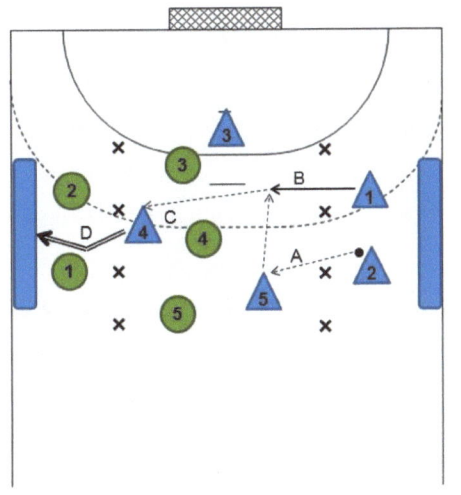

Course:
- Two teams play against each other.
- Two players of the defending team play in the goal zone.
- Throw-off is carried out from the goal zone (A). One of the goalkeepers (2) joins his team for playing the attack (B).
- Hence, the attacking team always is in numerical superiority.
- The team in ball possession tries to position a player in such a way that he can catch a pass (C) and shoot at the opponents' mat.
- The player must bounce the ball (D), i.e. the ball must touch the ground before it hits the mat.
- Both goalkeepers may try to save the ball.
- If the ball has bounced against the mat, the attacking team gets a point.
- The other team carries out a throw-off in the goal zone. One of the goalkeepers joins his team for playing the attack. One player of the team who is now playing defense joins the other goalkeeper in the goal zone.

Minihandball training and handball training for young kids

No.: M5		Defending		★★★	60
Opening part		**Main part**		**Final part**	
X	Warm-up/running		Ball handling/coordination	X	Closing game
	Running exercise		Passing and catching		Sprint contest
X	Short game		Dribbling		
	Coordination		Shooting		
	Sprint contest	X	Defending		
	Strengthening		Goalkeeper		
X	Ball familiarization	X	Applying contents in a game		

Key:

✗ Cone

△ Attacker/Player

● Defending player

▭ Small vaulting box

▦ Ball box

○ Hoop

▬ Foam noodles (foam beams)

Equipment required:
→ 8 cones, about 8 to 10 hoops, 6 foam noodles (foam beams), 2 small vaulting boxes, sufficient number of handballs

Description:
This training unit focuses on the positional play in the defense in a playful manner. Following the warm-up which focuses on reaction to external signs and legwork with quick changes of direction, stealing of the ball will be practiced through ball familiarization exercises. The subsequent defending exercise focuses on the blocking of running paths. A game in which the defending players play in a team focuses on the positional play between opponent and shooting target. The training unit is rounded off with a closing game.

The training unit consists of the following key exercises:
- Warm-up/running (5/5)
- Short game (10/15)
- Ball familiarization (10/25)
- Defending/legwork (10/35)
- Defending/team play (15/50)
- Closing game (10/60)

Training unit total time: 60 minutes

No.: M5-1	Warm-up/running	5	5

Course:
- The players form teams of 2.
- One player runs ahead while the other player follows at short distance.
- The second player guides his teammate by giving the following signs:
    - Patting on the right shoulder → Turn right.
    - Patting on the left shoulder → Turn left.
    - Patting on both shoulders → Stop.
    - Patting on both shoulders one more time → Start running again.
- Switch tasks after a while.

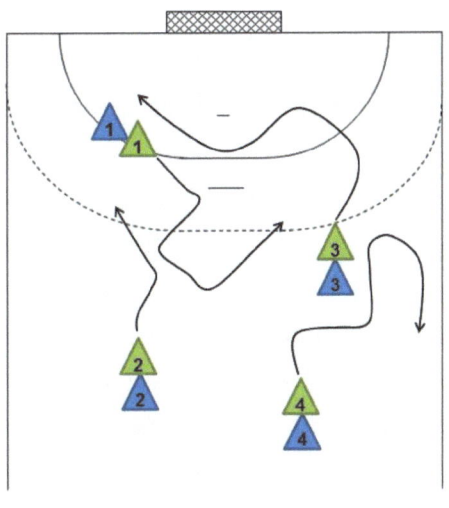

Variant:
- The player who runs ahead is wearing a blindfold.

No.: M5-2	Short game	10	15

Setting:
- Define a playing field with cones (or lines).

Course:
- Two players each lie on the floor next to each other.
- Two players stand in the field, one of them is the tagger (1), the other one is the runner (2).
- 1 tries to tag 2 (A).
- 2 runs away (B). If 2 lies down next to a pair on the floor (C), the player lying on the outer side (here

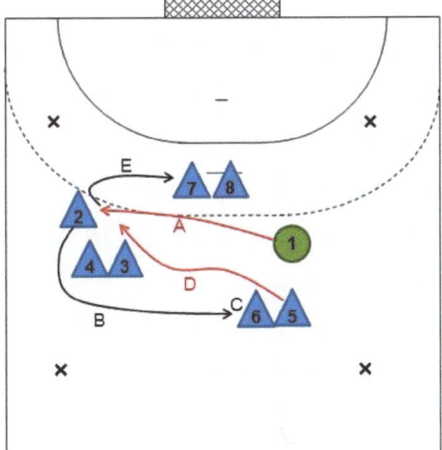

- 5) becomes the new tagger and now tries to tag 1 (D).
- 1 runs away (E) and now also may lie down next to a pair on the floor. And so on.
- If a player has been tagged before lying down next to a pair on the floor, the roles are switched immediately.

⚠ The players should adjust to the new situation quickly – the new tagger gets up immediately and the former tagger runs away.

⚠ The players should lie down next to a pair on the floor frequently in order to change the tagging players over and over again.

No.: M5-3	Ball familiarization	10	25

Course:
- The players sit down in a circle, except for two players (for larger groups, make two circles or define three defending players).
- The players sitting in the circle pass a ball (A and B).
- 1 and 2 try to steal the ball.
- If the defending players steal the ball or the ball gets lost, the player who has passed the ball takes over the position of the player who has been playing defense for a longer time.

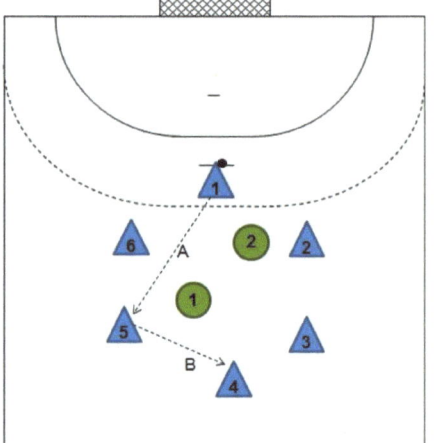

Variants:
- The players do not sit but stand in a circle. Only bounce passes are allowed.
- The players in the circle stand on one foot. No banana passes are allowed.

⚠ The defending players should work together.

⚠ The players must not steal the ball with their feet.

Minihandball training and handball training for young kids

No.: M5-4	Defending/legwork	10	35

Setting:
- Position hoops in a circle (at least one more hoop than players).

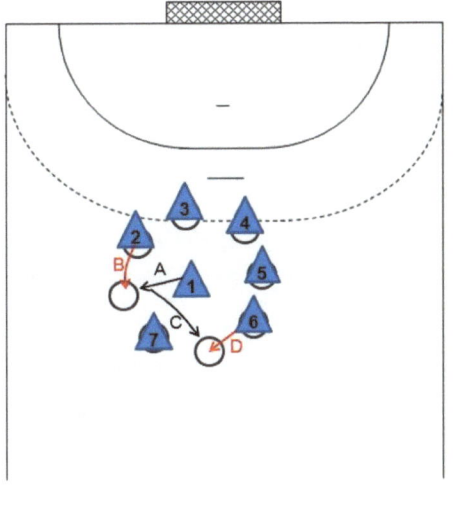

Course:
- The players stand in the hoops which lie in a circle.
- One player stands in the center of the circle without a hoop (1).
- 1 tries to step into one of the spare hoops (A).
- The other players try to avoid this by quickly sidestepping into the spare hoops in order to block them (B).
- Once a hoop has been blocked, 1 tries to step into another hoop (C). The other players try to avoid this through quick sidestepping (D).
- If 1 succeeds and steps into a hoop, his neighbor on the right now enters the center of the circle.

⚠ The players standing in the hoops should move on so that the player in the center cannot get a hoop.

⚠ Change the player in the center after about 10 attempts.

| No.: M5-5 | Defending/team play | 15 | 50 |

Setting:
- Pile up two small vaulting boxes.
- Put foam noodles (foam beams) on the floor so that they form a circle around the vaulting boxes. The players must not step into that circle.
- Define an outer circle with cones or more foam noodles at some meters' distance.

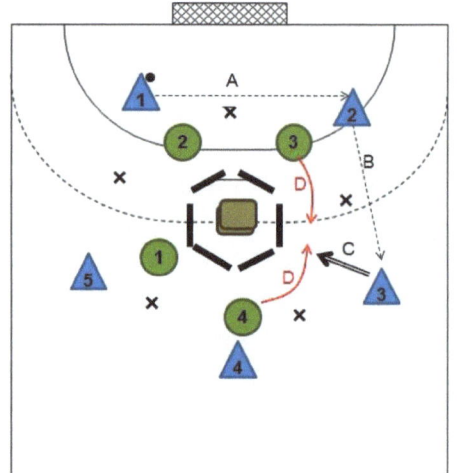

Course:
- Two teams play against each other.
- The attacking players stand outside of the cone circle and, through passing the ball (A and B), try to give one of their players the opportunity to shoot at the small vaulting boxes (C).
- If the player hits one of the boxes, the team gets a point.
- The defending players act in numerical inferiority. They must try to prevent the attacking players from hitting the boxes by positioning a defending player between the attacking player holding the ball and the vaulting boxes.
- As the defending players act in numerical inferiority, they must sidestep (D) in order to close the gaps.
- The players change the tasks after several attempts (at least one player must stay in the attacking team so that the attacking team still is in numerical superiority).

⚠ In the beginning, the attacking players may play passes to their neighboring teammates only. In the further course of the game, they also may play diagonal passes (e.g. from 1 to 3).

⚠ Consider playing with a foam ball, in order to take away the defending players' fear of getting hit.

⚠ The defending players should move on quickly (D) and step towards the player in ball possession, however, they should allow the passes of the attacking players (A, B).

| No.: M5-6 | Closing game | 10 | 60 |

Setting:
- Use cones to divide the playing field into several corridors (three corridors here).
- If there is only one goal available, use cones or poles to define the target zone (F).
- Make two teams. The players of each team stand in the different corridors in an even number, if possible (position fewer players in the center corridors, if necessary).

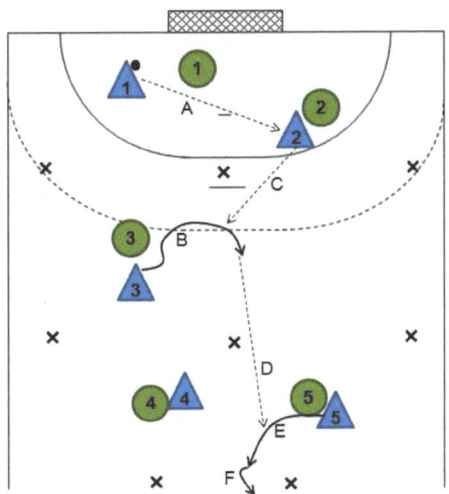

Course:
- The players try to put the ball in the goal (team 1) or in the cone goal on the other side (team 2).
- While doing this, the players must not leave their corridor, but rather pass the ball from one corridor to the next (C and D).
- Passes within one corridor (A) and return passes to the previous corridor are allowed as well.
- The players in the individual corridors must run to get rid of their opponent (B and E) so that they can play or catch a pass.
- If a team manages to put the ball into the target zone (F), the team gets a point. Now the other team may try to pass the ball through the corridors to the other side and get a point.
- Which team scores highest?

Variants:
- Allow bounce passes only.
- The attacking players in the center corridor act in numerical superiority to facilitate passing between the individual corridors (this variant is also suitable if there is an uneven number of players).

 Change the corridors and tasks regularly.

4. Printing template for planning the training unit

Description: Each exercise of the training unit can be planned using an individual sketch (blank playing field) and a written description.

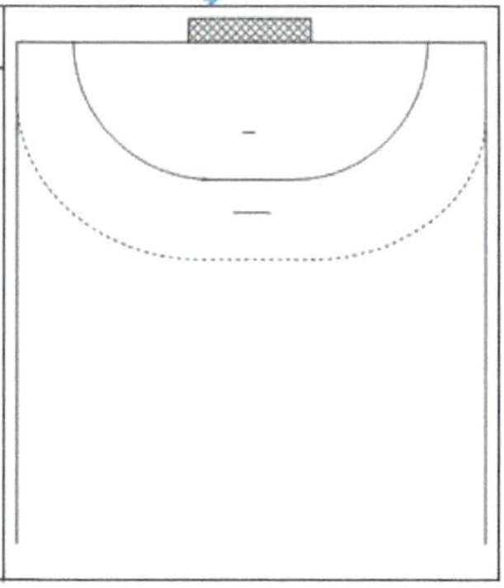

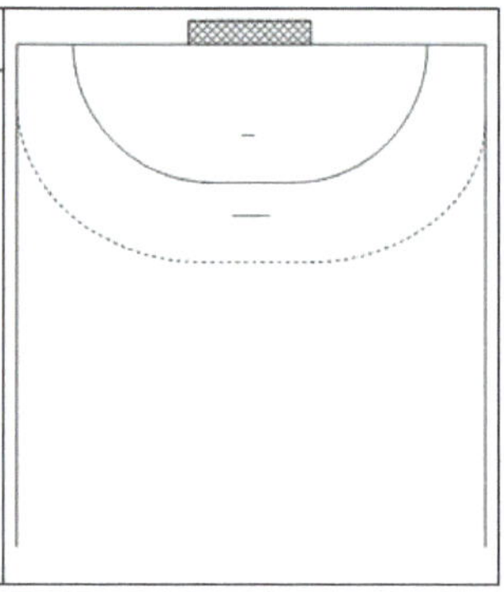

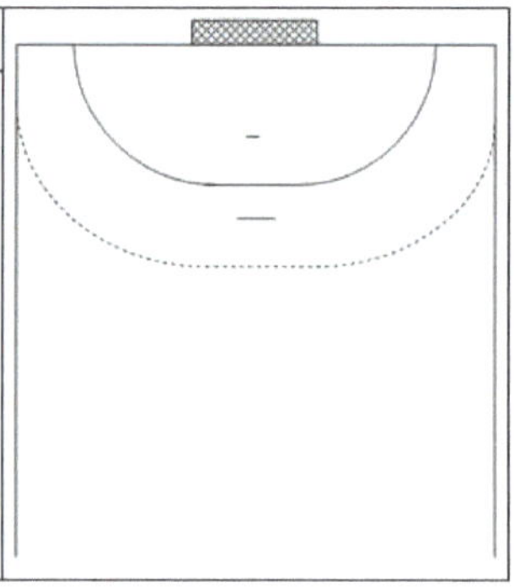

Free download and further templates at:
http://handball-uebungen.de/index.php/formulare

5. Editor's note

JÖRG MADINGER, born in Heidelberg (Germany) in 1970

July 2014 (further training): 3-day coaching workshop: "Basic components of goalkeeper training", held by the German Handball Association (Deutscher Handballbund, DHB)
Lecturers: Michael Neuhaus, Renate Schubert, Marco Stange, Norbert Potthoff, Olaf Gritz, Andreas Thiel, Henning Fritz

May 2014 (further training): 3-day coaching further training during the VELUX EHF Final4, held by the **German Handball Coaching Association (Deutsche Handball Trainer Vereinigung, DHTV)/DHB**
Lecturers: Jochen Beppler (DHB coach), Christian vom Dorff (DHB referee), Mark Dragunski (coach of TuSeM Essen, Germany),

Klaus-Dieter Petersen (DHB coach), Manolo Cadenas (coach of the Spanish national team)

May 2013 (further training): 3-day coaching further training during the VELUX EHF Final4, held by the **German Handball Coaching Association (Deutsche Handball Trainer Vereinigung, DHTV)/DHB**
Lecturers: Prof. Dr. Carmen Borggrefe (University of Stuttgart, Germany), Klaus-Dieter Petersen (DHB coach), Dr. Georg Froese (sports psychologist), Jochen Beppler (DHB base camp coach), Carsten Alisch (young talents' hockey coach)

Since July 2012: A-License, DHB

Since February 2011: Handball club trainings, coaching (training and competitive areas)

November 2011: Foundation of the Handball Specialist Publishing Company (Handball Fachverlag) (handball-uebungen.de, Handball Practice and Special Handball Practice)

May 2009: Foundation of the handball online platform handball-uebungen.de

2008-2010: Youth coordinator and youth coach, SG Leutershausen (Germany)

Since 2006: B-License

Editor's note

In 1995, a friend convinced me to join him in coaching a handball youth team (male, under 13 years of age).

This was the beginning of my career as a team handball coach. Ever since I enjoyed working as a coach and had high requirements concerning my exercises. Soon, the standard pool of exercises wasn't enough for me anymore and I started to modify and develop drills myself.

Today, I coach a broad range of youth and adult teams with different performance levels and adjust my training units to the individual needs of the teams.

A few years ago, I started selling my exercises and drills online at handball-uebungen.de. Since, in handball training, there is a tendency towards a general athletic training that focuses on coordination work – especially in the training of youth teams –, a large number of my games and exercises can be applied to other sports as well.

Get inspired by the various game concepts, be creative, and rely on your own experiences!

Yours sincerely,
Jörg Madinger

6. Further reference books published by DV Concept

From warm-up to handball team play – 75 exercises for every handball training unit
By making your training units more diverse, you can increase the players' motivation, since you consistently offer new approaches to improve and refine familiar movement sequences. In this book, you will find inspiring exercises you can apply during each phase of your everyday team handball training – from warm-up and goalkeeper warm-up shooting to the common contents of the main phase and the closing games. Each exercise is illustrated and described in an easy, comprehensible manner. Specific notes give you tips on what you need to be aware of.

This book deals with the following key subjects:

Warm-up:
- Basic warm-up
- Short warm-up games
- Sprint contests
- Coordination
- Ball familiarization
- Goalkeeper warm-up shooting

Basic exercises, basic play, and target play:
- Offense/series of shots
- General offense
- Fast throw-off
- 1st and 2nd wave
- Defensive action
- Closing games
- Endurance

At the end of this book, you will find an entire methodological training unit. The objective of this training unit is to improve shooting and quick decision-making under pressure.

Varied handball shooting drills – 60 exercises for every handball training unit
Shooting is a central component of team handball and must be practiced and improved regularly. Therefore, it is reasonable to integrate shooting series into training units from time to time. This collection of exercises contains 60 comprehensible practical drills focusing on this subject. They can be integrated in every training unit.

The exercises are divided into the following six categories and three difficulty levels (easy, medium, difficult):
- Technique
- Shooting at fixed targets
- Series of shots at the goal
- Shooting training for specific playing positions
- Complex series of shots
- Shooting competitions

With these options, you can easily make your shooting trainings more diverse and create new approaches for every age group. Additional notes and possible variations should inspire you to further modify the exercises and to adjust them to your players' level of performance.

Please also visit our online shop at www.handball-uebungen.de

www.ingramcontent.com/pod-product-compliance
Lightning Source LLC
Chambersburg PA
CBHW041803160426
43191CB00001B/27